Explaining to Someone Has Breast Cancer

Yvonne Crawley

DEDICATION

To those who have helped me on my journey. Thank you for your love and support, for being there when the tears were flowing, for an endless supply of dinners, all the home baked bread and cakes and the great variety of soups to build me up, for being an ear to complain or a cinema trip to distract me, for all the kind words of encouragement and involvement in fundraising but especially for sharing this journey with me.

I 💜 my family.

1.

Mammy is
Worried!

2.

She has a sore boobie.

3.

The doctor
says mammy
has breast
cancer.

4.

Mammy is upset but the whole family still loves her.

5.

Mammy gets
special medicine
called
chemotherapy to
kill cancer cells.

6.

Chemotherapy makes mammy sick.

7.

Chemotherapy makes
mammy's hair fall out.

8.

She is bald like the baby.

9.

It's ok. Mammy can wear a pretty hat or a wig.

10.

Mammy is
very tired.

11.   She sleeps a lot.

Soon mammy's hair
begins to grow.

12.

Mammy now needs an operation. She is scared.

13.

The doctor
takes the
sick boobie in
an operation.

14.

Mammy lives in hospital for a few days.

15.

Mammy wears a sponge boobie.
I call it her pretend boob.

16.

Mammy goes to the hospital everyday for radiotherapy.

17.

The radiotherapy machine kills cancer cells.

18.

Mammys skin is sore and pink. She must exercise her arm.

19.

Mammy is smiling
now. No more
breast cancer.
Her hair is still
growing. Yippee!

20.

Mammy has another operation. The doctor gives her a new boobie.

21.

When mammy was sick I was afraid, but she always loves me.

22.

We are a happy family again.

My name is
_____ and
I love my
mammy.

24.

For parents faced with the difficult
question of a breast cancer diagnosis
and who have children.

Made in the USA
Columbia, SC
19 June 2022

61947752R00018